God's World Nature Poems

Sandy Bohon LMHC

Dedication

This book is dedicated to my granddaughter,
Katie, who inspired me to illustrate.

God's World

God is not in the rain
That hits my windowpane,
Or in the clouds above
But He sends us His Love.

God is not rocks or trees
Small ponds or raging seas,
Nor hills or mountains high
Or rainbows in the sky.

And if you look outside
You'll see the world so wide,
Tigers and birds that sing
God has made everything.

How Wonderful Am I

Once was an inchworm,
Crawling along,
Content as could be
Singing his song.

"All of my friends are
So very fast,
But I see all details
As I inch past."

Then up in the sky
    Flew a large bird,
Soaring and singing
    His song could be heard.

"I'm so high up that,
    Rivers I see,
Mountains and forests
    Pass right under me."

So, if you're an inchworm
    Or a bird in the sky
God wants everyone to sing
    "How wonderful am I."

Love is Like the Ocean

Love is like the ocean
It's depths cannot be known
But we can see
The gentle waves,
Upon the beach are blown.

God Loves All

The stillness of the pond
The raging of the sea,
The blooming of a rose -
And God made me.

The thundering in the storm
The sky so wide and blue,
The beauty of a butterfly -
And God made you.

The coldness in the winter
Leaves changing in the fall
The sun above so bright -
And God loves all.

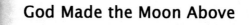

God Made the Moon Above

God made the moon above
    And the stars to shine at night.
By day He made the sun to rise,
    To give us heat and light.

God made the rain to fall,
    To water the plants and trees,
God made the cats and dogs,
    And butterflies, birds, and bees.

Everthing you see was made,
    By God up high above,
And He wants you to know
    He also sends His love.

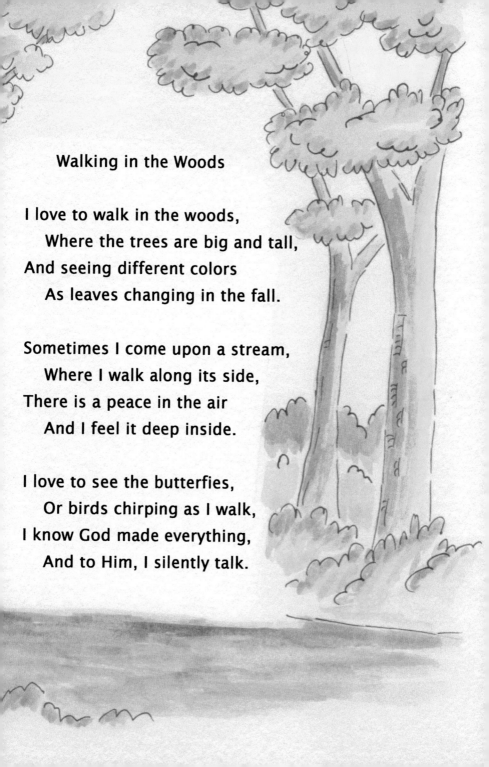

Walking in the Woods

I love to walk in the woods,
  Where the trees are big and tall,
And seeing different colors
  As leaves changing in the fall.

Sometimes I come upon a stream,
  Where I walk along its side,
There is a peace in the air
  And I feel it deep inside.

I love to see the butterfies,
  Or birds chirping as I walk,
I know God made everything,
  And to Him, I silently talk.

Garden - Weed

My Father above
    Made the trees
And the flowers
    That feed the bees.

He made the grass
    For the cows to feed,
And my garden
    Full of weed.

I pulled them out
    One by one,
Didn't rest till,
    My work was done.

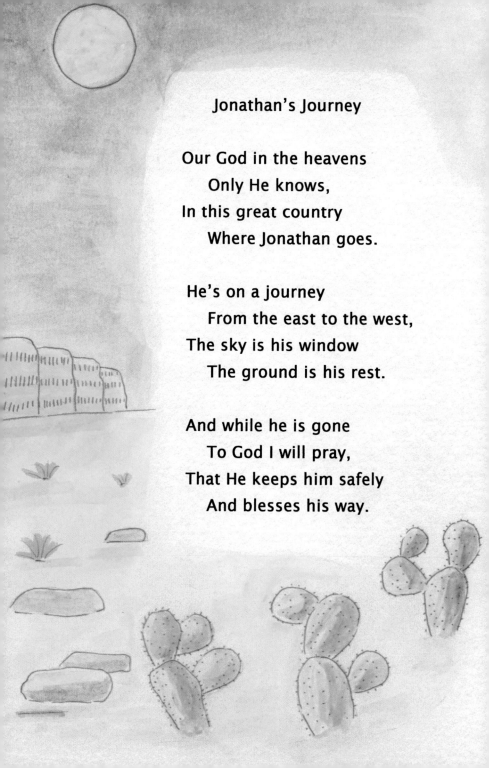

Jonathan's Journey

Our God in the heavens
   Only He knows,
In this great country
   Where Jonathan goes.

He's on a journey
   From the east to the west,
The sky is his window
   The ground is his rest.

And while he is gone
   To God I will pray,
That He keeps him safely
   And blesses his way.

Thunderstorm

I saw the storm
   Coming my way
One hot and humid
   Summer day.
The sky turned dark
   The clouds deep gray,
Out on the swing
   We could not play.
So, into the house
   We had to stay
Until the storm
   Passed far away.

The Moon That Shines

The moon that shines above tonight
Is shining over you,
And looking up I see its light
Is shining on me too.

The Pond

I went out to the pond today
　To see what I could find,
My friend came along to play,
　My sister we left behind.

Some ducks were swimming around
　They saw us, away they flew,
As they went homeward bound,
　Up in the sky so blue.

We saw some minnows swimming past,
　With our nets, we swooshed a lot,
Though they were so very fast,
　Many fish we still had caught.

Next time to the pond we'll bring,
　Our poles out far we'll cast,
And if we don't catch anything,
　Friendships we've made will last.

Salvation

I am so happy
Can't you see,
Because I have Jesus
Living in me.

I have believed
He died for me
I'll be with Him,
All eternity.

"For God so loved the world that
He gave His one and only Son, that
whoever believes in Him shall not
perish but have eternal life."
(John 3:16 NIV)

Psalm 23

The Lord is my Shepherd, I lack nothing. He makes me lie down in green pastures, He leads me beside quiet waters, He refreshes my soul. He guides me along the right paths for His names's sake.

Even though I walk through the darkest valley, I will fear no evil, for You are with me; Your rod and Your staff, they comfort me.

You prepare a table before me in the presence of my enemies. You anoint my head with oil, my cup overflows.

Surely Your goodness and love will follow me all the days of my life, and I will dwell in the house of the Lord forever.

I Did Not Create

I did not create the stars above
  Nor the moon that shines at night
The galaxies in outer space,
  Or the sun that gives us light.

I did not create my little dog
  Or my cat that sleeps all day,
The grass or trees outside
  And my friends that like to play.

God made the Heavens and Earth
  And He is Lord over all,
Jesus loves me very much,
  Although I'm oh, so, small!

The Singing Bird

I wish I was a bird,
　　Flying in the air,
I'd be up so high,
　　Without a care.

I'd see children below,
　　Smiling up at me
Playing at the beach,
　　Is what I'd see.

They're building castles,
   In the sand,
The best ones ever,
   In all the land.

And in the clouds,
   I want to fly,
Singing to Jesus
   As I pass by.

The World's so Big

The world's so big
  And I'm so small,
The mountains large
  And fir trees tall.
The flowers wave
  Among the weeds,
And both are blown
  New life of seeds.
The lions roar
  While tigers pounce,
And streams flow free
  Glistening with dance.
And God does watch
  From up above
And showers us all,
  With His love.

Clouds

I saw a dragon in the clouds,
   His head so fierce and mean
Who swiftly turned into a horse
   His body so fast and lean.

Then over there I saw a cat,
   Whose mouth was open wide,
And I think I saw a little mouse
   Who quickly ran to hide.

Tomorrow I'll go out again,
   To see what the clouds may bring
For they are limited to my mind
   And can make most anything.

NATURE

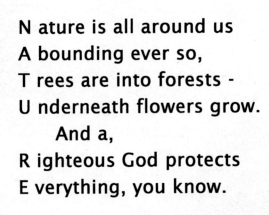

N ature is all around us
A bounding ever so,
T rees are into forests -
U nderneath flowers grow.
    And a,
R ighteous God protects
E verything, you know.

God speaks to us through His Bible and through nature. Being out in nature is awesome and relaxing. The Bible speaks about how God created the heavens and earth, and He created it for us to enjoy.

God gave us the Bible so that we can learn about Him and His will for our lives. It also speaks about how we are all sinners, and from the creation of the world, God prepared a way to restore fellowship that was broken from Adam and Eves sin.

Jesus came to earth to die on the cross for our sins in our place. Salvation is trusting in the payment that Christ made on the cross in our place. When you trust Jesus as your Savior, as a free gift, you can spend eternity with Him.

"I write these things to you who believe in the name of the Son of God so that you may know that you have eternal life." (1John 5:13)

ABOUT THE AUTHOR

Sandy Bohon is a Licensed Mental Health Counselor practicing in central Florida. She received her bachelor's degree from Florida Bible College and a Master of Counseling degree from Liberty University. In her spare time, Sandy enjoys spending time with her family, going to the beach and gardening. She has three adult children, three grandchildren and a rescue puppy, Bailey.

Other books by Sandy Bohon available on Amazon:
JOY in Overcoming Depression Through God's Word
JOY in Knowing Jesus Through God's Word
Poetry and Devotions for the SOUL
Poetry and Devotions for the SOUL for Youth

For more information please contact me:
sandybohonlmhc@gmail.com
And join my mailing list at:
www.sandybohonlmhc.com

If you enjoyed this book please leave a review on Amazon. Thanks!

Made in the USA
Monee, IL
08 May 2022